In the Nest

With thanks to Dr. S. James Reynolds, University of Birmingham,
for information about birds and nests.
Edited by Gillian Doherty and Jenny Tyler.

In the Nest

Anna Milbourne

Illustrated by Laurence Cleyet-Merle

Designed by Laura Fearn and Laura Parker

All day long, a little bird
flies to and fro.

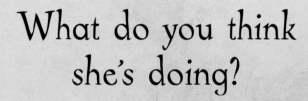

What do you think
she's doing?

She's carrying twigs to the cherry tree.

She weaves the twigs
around and around
to make a tidy nest.

Then she lays five speckled eggs inside,
and snuggles up to keep them warm.

Tucked away inside the nest,
the little bird's eggs are safe from harm.

A hungry fox would like
to gobble them up.

But he can't
reach that high.

There's another nest in the cherry tree.

It's hidden away
inside the trunk.

And there's one in the muddy riverbank too.

The little bird sits on her eggs and waits.

She doesn't leave the nest –
not even when she's hungry.

The father bird brings
seeds for her to eat.

One day there's a...

tap   tap   tap

Quickly, the little bird
hops off the nest.

The first tiny baby cracks out of his egg.

He doesn't look
much like a bird.

His eyes are shut tight, and
he doesn't have a single feather.

All the other babies hatch out too.

They open their beaks wide
and SQUAWK for food.

Their mother and father
bring juicy bugs.

The babies gulp them down
and SQUAWK for more.

Soon, the baby birds grow fluffy feathers.
They open their eyes and look around.

They grow **bigger** and **bigger**...

until they're much too
squashed in the little nest.

One of the babies flaps his wings.

He flaps
and flaps...

but he doesn't take off.

So he jumps off the nest
and flaps some more.

He's flying for
the very first time!

Before long, the other
baby birds start flying too.

They swoop and soar...

up, up
and away.

All the little birds
have gone.

But maybe one will
come back next year.